A Voice For The Redwoods

by
Loretta Halter

Illustrated by
Peter Bartczak

Published by
Nature's Hopes & Heroes
Boulder Creek, California

ACKNOWLEDGEMENTS

I wish to give special thanks, first to John Tucker Osgood, my husband, muse, and editor, for his constant support, insight, dedication to, and belief in my work. I also wish to give special thanks to Peter Bartczak, for his passion and sensitivity, who made my story come alive through his art; and who also, along with his wife, Victoria, gave me great encouragement throughout the process of producing this second edition of this book. I want to also give many thanks to Jim Mullen, and to his apprentice Virginia Gavel, designers and consultants for this book, who worked closely and enthusiastically with both Peter and me. Lastly, I wish to give thanks to all the environmental groups who work so hard to protect and preserve our forests, for future generations to enjoy and cherish.

Publisher:

Nature's Hopes & Heroes
www.natureshopesandheroes.com
Boulder Creek, California

ISBN 978-0-9822942-0-8

Printed in China through Palace Press International
2nd Printing

Printed on Recycled Paper

Special Notes: 10% of the author's proceeds from the sale of this book will be donated to environmental organizations. It is the policy of Palace Press International that for every tree used to produce the printing of this book, two new trees were planted.

DEDICATION

To Victoria,

Peter

and Eyesa,

wise, gentle muses.

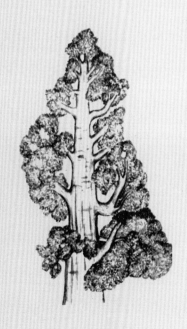

INTRODUCTION

Consider the Life of Trees

Consider the life of trees.

Aside from the axe, what trees acquire from man is inconsiderable.

What man may acquire from trees is immeasurable.

From their mute forms there flows a poise, in silence;

A lovely sound and motion in response to the wind.

What peace comes to those aware of the voice and bearing of these trees!

Trees do not scream for attention.

A tree, a rock, has no pretense, only a real growth out of itself,

In close communion with the universal spirit.

A tree retains a deep serenity.

It establishes in the earth not only its root system but also

Those roots of its beauty and its unknown consciousness.

Sometimes one may sense a glisten of that consciousness, and with

Such perspective, feel that man is not necessarily the highest form of life.

— Cedric Wright

They Commune

They commune on high, the redwoods,

As all who rise in lush, green splendor

Commune

In the invisible air

On high—

Be very still,

At night especially,

And in the gathering of silence these mountains

Provide,

You can hear the intense hum

Of the dark masses of their towering crowns

Overhead,

Engaged in centuries-long interweaving conversations,

Expanding out to such open, abundant, even further

Reaching space—

They are closer to the stars than we realize.

So much,

If we could but find that one Thread

That draws us into the weave,

So much they could tell—

—Ron Lampi

◈ Chapter I ◈

Late in the autumn, a strong wind carried aloft thousands of tiny winged seeds from the seed cones of redwood trees. Then, after being released from the wind's grip, the seeds drifted softly to the forest floor.

Many of the seeds began to germinate soon after falling; but most of them died, because they could not penetrate the thick layer of decaying leaves and branches covering the ground. Others died soon after sprouting, since the forest floor contained a fungus that preyed upon the tender roots of these redwood seedlings. Others could not survive under the thick canopy of trees where they couldn't receive enough sunlight.

While the vast majority of seeds perished, a miracle nevertheless occurred. One tiny seed, smaller than a grain of sand, came in contact with moist soil minerals. From this seed sprang a little seedling which eventually poked its head above ground, drawn to warm sunlight filtering through the tall, ancient redwood trees.

When the little seedling took her first look at this world around her, she was struck most by the sight of these wondrous trees! She considered herself so insignificant, so puny and frail, compared to these trees.

"Who are these mighty creatures? Who and what am I?" she wondered as she looked around. To the left of her stood a huge growth of sword ferns, with fronds that curved gracefully towards the ground, like the necks of swans.

"I must be one of these lovely creatures, since I am growing so very close to them. But," she paused, "My leaves are not quite like theirs."

She examined her own leaves more carefully as she compared herself to the fronds of the sword fern and noticed how well formed the ferns' leaves were. "Well," she thought, "I'm still young yet. In time I will grow and change, and become as lovely as they are. But in the meantime, I'm just glad to be alive." She looked up once more at the giant trees that stood nearby, and somehow felt so secure and peaceful in their presence.

ᵔᵉᵒ Chapter II ᵒᵉᵛ

A month passed. The temperatures grew more and more chilly, the days grew shorter and shorter, but the Sun's rays continued to touch the seedling's stubby needle-like leaves, urging her to grow closer to the source of this warm and comforting light.

While she was slowly developing, there was a collar of dormant buds surrounding her that, little by little, she grew to appreciate; for when browsing deer came by to nibble, this collar of buds acted as a hedge to protect her from being eaten. With this added protection, she could continue to grow. The gracefully leaning ferns still hung high over her, but somehow they didn't look quite so tall anymore. "Soon," she thought confidently, "I, too, will grow tall enough to lean over in an arch, and my leaves will lengthen out to be as comely as theirs."

But as the wind blew, she looked up towards the redwood trees that towered above her, closer to the heavenly light. She could not even see the tops of these magnificent beings, only their lower branches, and thick, wide trunks whose bark swirled around them in an upward spiral like sacred pillars. She looked longingly at them and, if she could have sighed, she would have.

Suddenly she was distracted by a peculiar sound that she had not heard before. Over the past month she had become accustomed to the many sounds of this dense forest. She knew the cries of the red-tailed hawk, and of the Steller's jays during the day; and the calls of the pygmy owl and of the spotted owl at dusk. She knew the husky, powerful walk of the grizzly bear and the hushed steps of the elegant black-tailed deer. She also could distinguish the sounds of opossums and raccoons at night, while during the day she was quite familiar with the high-energy scamperings of chipmunks and squirrels. And while a whole chorus of different songbirds could be heard throughout the forest, the young seedling

could also detect the steps of the tiny shrew as it preyed voraciously on a variety of delectable insects.

She had come to know so many special sounds, but this sound—this sound—which was growing clearer and more distinct as it drew close, was unfamiliar to her. It was steady, evenly paced, sure-footed, quiet, and yet not nearly as quiet as the bobcat.

At last the seedling discovered who made the curious sounds: for the first time in her life, she saw humans. There were two of them walking together, side by side. One of them was rather thin and tall, but bent over in an arch like the graceful fern. The other, who was carrying a basket, was much smaller by comparison, but straight and strong.

These two humans came to stop right next to the little seedling.

Their backs were turned to her as they gazed at an especially large and ancient redwood tree standing before them. It was this same tree that the young seedling often gazed at in awe and admiration. "They must feel the same way as I," she thought.

"How did the life of these redwood trees begin, Great-grandmother?" the smaller human asked, as he set down the basket and rejoined his great-grandmother in looking upon the giant redwood with solemn respect.

"Hmm," the taller human responded thoughtfully. "The creation of our world is shrouded in mystery. You have heard our story of Creation since the day you were born—of how, long ago, there was a fight between good and evil, followed by a devastating flood, which wiped out all traces of previous life. All was destroyed except Coyote. He was alone for a long time until, at last, the great eagle and swift hummingbird joined him. Then later, through Coyote, all life sprang into its wondrous magnificence."

"But how did Coyote make the trees?"

"I honestly don't know, child. None of our stories speak of how Coyote actually made these trees."

7

But let me tell you some stories I learned through our ancestors. Years before you or I were born, our ancestors hunted and gathered food just as we do now. As they searched for food, they met many people who exchanged goods with them. Through celebrations of dance and song, they also exchanged Creation stories.

"Among the stories that were translated and handed down, there are two that stand out in my memory. The first

was told by the Tolowa people. It was explained in their story that the Creator stood poised amidst rushing waters while envisioning the world into existence. It came floating in from the south with a single redwood tree in the very center.

"In the second story, told by the Chastacosta people, they gave the Creator the name Howalachi, which means Giver. Howalachi stood with his unnamed companion and dearest friend. Together,

8

they stood and waited on the ancient waters. Then, the heavy darkness that surrounded the waters eventually lifted and folded until an island became visible. The island came floating out of the east and glistened radiantly; the way pure white snow does under the sun.

"On this gleaming white island there stood two trees. The first was a redwood tree and the second, an ash. The Creator Howalachi smiled upon these two trees and then blew tobacco smoke over them so that they began to bud. Then rain came and fell to the ground, causing grass to shoot up. While the rainwaters swelled into great oceans, the Creator made five cakes of mud and dropped them, one by one, into the ocean. Slowly, these cakes rose and joined each other at the surface of the waters, thus forming the whole world."

"Five mud cakes?" the smaller human asked in puzzlement.

"Yes, my son. These cakes each symbolized the five steps of change involved in the Creation cycle. The Earth underwent five major changes in order to become habitable for all living creatures. And as the Earth passed through each change, it grew in so many ways that it was able to promote

9

and carry on the cycles of life."

The smaller human nodded contemplatively. "So both these stories show that the redwood trees have been here, since near the very beginning of time. It's as if they have always been here."

"Yes," the great-grandmother smiled. "They have been here for a very long time—since the beginning of Creation. But come. We must leave this holy ground. It is too sacred to stay in here long. The spirit of the grizzly bear is the guardian of this temple, day and night, so we must be quick."

The young human lifted the large basket full of acorns to carry as the two started to leave. But before heading off, the older, taller human turned to face the little seedling, so that now both humans were looking down at her. "Ah! A seedling among these ferns," the elder one said, hunching over,

closer to the seedling so she could touch her leaves. The seedling, in turn, got a close look at this human's face. It had many deep grooves and creases drawn across a dark and ruddy complexion so that, to the seeding, this human looked much like an ancient redwood tree—except, its face was lit up by two warm, brown eyes that glistened in the sun.

"Someday," the great-grandmother spoke softly, "you will grow to be a great one, too."

"Me? A great one, too?" The seedling smiled inside. She only wished the two humans could have stayed longer. She enjoyed listening to their interesting voices, and to the strange and beautiful stories they told.

The young seedling looked up once more at the great tree that stood before her, and wondered.

Chapter III

After a series of rainstorms passed, springtime came in with a flutter of bird and butterfly wings. There was a busy excitement in the air.

The little seedling had grown a little over a foot, so that now she was a sapling, nearly as tall as the ferns about her. But, still, she maintained her awkward, somewhat irregular shape. She also wondered about the new growth of ferns that uncoiled into large, graceful arches. Feeling somewhat disconcerted about this, she wondered if she might be a defective fern, and yet she could not stay feeling worried for long. With all this new life buzzing and blooming around her, she couldn't help but rejoice. Once again, she felt an overwhelming gladness in being alive. She felt as alive as the box elder and big leaf maple trees that were no longer winter barren, but now were lush with fresh green leaves.

As the spring months unfurled into summer, Douglas irises, rhododendron and leopard lilies bloomed nearby with other flowers, adding a rich array of color to the forest carpet. Among them was the showy sight of the huge, creamy white and yellow western azalea blooms, which filled the air with such a sweet fragrance that the bees couldn't help but dance dizzily around them.

The little sapling watched with delight as each living form grew and blossomed with her. She watched, observing how the animals of the forest courted others of their species, and then later, weeks after mating, some gave birth to young, and raised them.

One warm evening, she watched a small grizzly cub wander from its den inside the hollow of a fallen fir tree. Its mother had lumbered off to forage for food earlier that evening and hadn't returned yet. As the cub sniffed around for its mama, a chattering squirrel distracted it. Then, as two jays cackled excitedly in a tree nearby, the small bear

wheeled around to face a large mountain lion. The cub turned to run back to its den, but the mountain lion lunged and grabbed the cub's back leg between its claws. It was about to sink its teeth into the cub's neck, when it heard a thundering roar from the mother bear.

She galloped towards her cub, and now only a few feet away, outstretched her large paw and swung a heavy blow down on the left flank of the mountain lion. The lion let out a piercing cry as it released the cub, and leapt out of reach of the mother bear's jaws. It took off running with a raging bear in hot pursuit. The mother grizzly was about to swing another heavily clawed blow, when the large cat dodged to the left, coming within inches of the sapling herself! It leapt with ease right over her, and continued racing another thirty feet, until it scrambled up the nearest branch of a big leaf maple. Then it shimmied up towards the next branch, when the bear lifted its massive body in an attempt to reach the lion. The seedling could feel the vibrations of the bear's angry roar as it paced around the tree. After some time, the mother grizzly finally gave up

and returned quickly to her cub, while the treed mountain lion licked its wound. The little seedling trembled with the wind as she considered her first lesson in the way many animals must fight to eat and to protect their young.

Later that summer, as the sapling studied twin fawns prancing after their mother, she was distracted by a sound she had heard once before. It was the sound of the two humans who had come last year in the early fall. She wondered if they would remember her. Would they recognize her since she had grown?

The two humans stopped at the same spot they had come to last fall, standing between the giant redwood and young sapling.

She was glad to see them, but noticed that the older human had grown more gaunt since their last visit. And yet, to the sapling, this human was something beautiful—bent forward like a thin and graceful fern, but having red and heavily lined skin similar to the bark of the redwood tree. This creature must be a human redwood fern, she finally decided. "So I shall call her Redwoodfern," she thought with satisfaction.

As the two humans turned to look at the sapling, the younger human cried out enthusiastically, "Look! Look Great-grandmother! Remember this tiny seedling?" The young human with sparkling eager eyes smiled, supporting his great-grandmother as she stooped down to get a closer view of the seedling.

"Chipmunk," she smiled back at her great-grandson affectionately. "Chipmunk, my son, we can no longer call this a seedling. It is a young tree now, a sapling, growing tall and strong just as you are. It is a young tree, just as you are a young man."

As Chipmunk beamed at both his great-grandmother and the young tree, Redwoodfern looked down the slope just a few feet beyond the tree where clear fresh water flowed from a small spring.

"Ah," she said. "I'll refill our water skins while you gather some more huckleberries."

While Chipmunk nimbly gathered handfuls of the tiny fruit and dropped them into a basket, Redwoodfern took their skins to the water. As she filled them, she began to recite a poem taught to her long ago by her father. The young tree listened carefully.

"The beauty of the trees,
The softness of the air,
The fragrance of the grass,
Speaks to me.
The summit of the mountain,
The thunder of the sky,
The rhythm of the sea,
Speaks to me.
The faintness of the stars,
The freshness of the morning,
The dewdrop on the flower,
Speaks to me.
The strength of fire,
The taste of salmon,
The trail of the Sun,
And the life that never goes away,
They speak to me.
And my heart soars."

✌ Chapter IV ✌

By the end of the summer, the young tree had grown another foot taller. She spread her shallow roots further out under the forest floor until she felt something very remarkable begin to happen to her. She felt someone else's roots touch her own. Of course, she had always felt all kinds of roots from various plants underneath and all around her own, but these roots felt stronger and wider. They linked up and curled around her own and, as the wind blew so that her body bent back, she was able to look up and acknowledge whose roots they were. They belonged to the ancient and stately tree that stood before her.

A tingling sensation shot all the way up her thin trunk. Was it the water and minerals she was pulling up through her roots? Or was it the sensation of joy she felt through an extension of friendship coming from this lofty tree?

She responded gratefully, curling her own roots and intertwining them around those of her ancient neighbor.

Chapter V

Summer drew to a close. The weather grew ever cooler, so that a number of plants started to die back, and even the late flowering plants lost their blooms. The leaves from the deciduous trees responded to the changing season, turning their colors to yellow, orange, and crimson. But these leaves soon lost their grip on the branches that once held them secure. With the first cold winds, they drifted to the forest floor. And though the redwoods, as well as the tan oaks, Douglas firs, and some other trees of the redwood community, were evergreen, they too began to shed old needles and leaves in the strengthening winds of autumn.

The young tree noticed that not as many animals roamed the forest as before. While many became less active, others, especially birds, began to migrate to warmer places the tree could never see.

The forest seemed so much emptier and quieter now, but the young tree did not feel alone. She could not possibly feel alone with her roots intertwined with those of the great redwood tree across from her, as well as with the roots of the slightly less gigantic redwood trees that stood near her in a circle.

As she gazed with contentment at all these towering trees, she remembered something that Redwoodfern had told Chipmunk last time they visited the forest. It was something she had said as the two of them left the forest. Redwoodfern had taken hold of Chipmunk's shoulders and made him turn to view all the redwood trees surrounding them. "Learn from these trees, my son. Like these trees, we must be a network of friends, a close family, who join forces, to stand up against any element that works to destroy us. It is through this intertwining of hearts, that we, like these trees intertwining their roots, gain a living foothold into eternity."

The young tree didn't quite understand the meaning of these words, but again she continued for days to think about what Redwoodfern had said. Then her thoughts were abruptly distracted by an onslaught of rainstorms that continued for weeks.

As the soil became more saturated with water, the young tree grew more frightened. She wondered whether or not she would be washed away with the runoff of excess water. Would her grip weaken around the roots of the larger trees? Like all redwood trees, her roots were shallow, but because she was young, they did not extend out very far yet. She knew amid the high winds and floodwaters, that her life was in jeopardy.

Suddenly she heard a piercing crack across the fast-filling river just eighty feet away from where she stood. A very tall redwood tree on the side of a hill toppled over, bringing down another redwood with it so that both went crashing down the hill.

The young tree shivered, but continued to cling through her roots to the support given her by the surrounding redwoods, and they, in turn held fast and securely to each other and to her.

The young tree observed how some of the plants near her became so inundated with water and sediment that they began to suffocate and die. She feared the same thing would happen to her, but as the rains continued steadily to pour, she remained saturated and weakened, but alive and safe.

Then suddenly, in the midst of these winter storms, two things occurred to her. She fully realized now that she was not a fern, but a tree, just as Redwoodfern had said. But more than that, she was a redwood tree! And with these realizations also came the understanding of Redwoodfern's words. Sustained through the floods and winds by her neighbors' roots clinging to her own, the young tree now understood the meaning of family and friendship.

Chapter VI

Spring came again. The little tree was happy to see the return of many birds that had gone south for the winter. She was also glad to see the flowering plants begin to bloom prolifically. And as they grew, she felt her own self grow. In fact, she felt strange changes taking place inside, as well as all over the surface of her body.

For one thing, now that she had shot up to well over four feet tall, she could no longer get enough water from her root system to all her needle-like leaves. So an important shift had to take place within her. She could feel her leaves pulling water up from her roots, through the channels in her trunk and branches.

The young tree felt other things happening to her body. In fact, she was delighted to see that she was beginning to look more like a redwood tree! Of course, she still had a long way to go before she could even compare herself to the stately beauty of these adult trees. Even so, she was quite excited about a layer of bark that developed around her as extra skin for protection. It protected her cambium, a thin circle of living cells underneath.

What she didn't know yet, but would come to learn, in time, was that each year she would grow a new layer of bark. With each year's new layer of bark, there would also be new wood called sapwood. Through this sapwood, the transpirational pull of the leaves would draw water and nutrients from the soil, to her outermost leaves.

Heartwood

**Xylem cells
or Sapwood**

**Cambium
layer**

Phloem

21

Chapter VII

Seasons came and went. The young tree continued to grow. She survived each stormy season and flourished afterwards from the generous doses of rain. She also continued to feel grateful for the support provided by the redwood trees around her, whose roots kept her anchored during the worst storms.

One hot, early autumn day, as she reflected on the gratitude she felt towards her fellow redwoods, she thought of her two human friends, Redwoodfern and Chipmunk. Five years had passed since she last saw them, and she longed to see them again.

At last, four days later, she at least got to see her friend Chipmunk. He came on this hot summer day to refresh himself underneath the cool shade of the redwood trees.

Chipmunk had grown quite tall and lanky. He looked strong and healthy, and walked with a proud, happy gait. He arrived between the giant redwood tree and the young tree, just as Redwoodfern and he used to do. He set down his basket which was full of a fresh catch of salmon. Then lowering his eyes, he began to thank Mother Earth for all her goodness and abundance shown to his people. Then wiping tears from his eyes, he also gave thanks for the great-grandmother who had taught him so many things.

He raised his head, his eyes, to the very height of the great tree, and breathed in deeply, exhaled slowly. Then once more he began to express his appreciation for life through the words his great-grandmother spoke while she was alive on Earth.

"Earth mother, star mother,
You who are called by
A thousand names,
May all remember?
We are cells in your body
And dance together.

You are the grain
And the loaf
That sustains us each day,
And as you are patient
With our struggles to learn,
So shall we be patient
With each other and ourselves.

We are radiant light
And sacred dark
—The balance—
You are the embrace that heartens
And the freedom beyond fear.

Within you we are born
We grow, live, and die—
You bring us around the circle
To rebirth,
Within us you dance
Forever."

As Chipmunk spoke, a gust of wind blew through the forest, making the great redwood trees creak and sway as if responding to the young man's words. And the young tree joined these ancient ones of the forest, swaying happily in the wind.

Chipmunk then turned to face the young redwood. "Young tree, you are my brother. In spirit we are kin. Both of us will continue to grow strong."

Brother? The tree wondered at this term. Whatever it meant, she understood it was a special word. And, somehow, though not linked by roots, she still felt a connection with this young man.

Chapter VIII

Just after Chipmunk spoke to the young redwood, he turned to face the direction of laughter coming his way. Then he began to chuckle as another young man, close to his age, called out to tease him.

"Oh, there you are. Hiding out here to get out of work, huh?"

Several tanned, reddish-skinned humans like Chipmunk, came to visit the forest this day. They came to gather acorns from the tan oak trees growing in among the redwoods. But they came to gather food more as an excuse to escape the heat. In fact, they started coming more frequently during the hot summer months, since the redwood forest provided them with a cool, damp atmosphere. The dampness came from the morning fog that gave way to midday heat, and from the great trees as they released water vapor from their leaves.

The young redwood was pleased that Chipmunk and his friends also seemed to enjoy the moisture of the forest, and yet she observed that they never stayed in the forest for very long. It wasn't until years later that she grew to understand why these humans, who called themselves the Ohlone people, seldom visited the redwood forest. She learned that they held the redwood trees in such reverence that to live among them would be as wrong as living in a church or temple. She also knew that they feared attack from the powerful grizzly bears that roamed the forest. As she acknowledged and respected their fear, she recalled Redwoodfern once telling Chipmunk that the spirit of the grizzly bear was guardian of the sacred forest.

Chapter IX

Thirty years passed. All seemed calm and predictable until one day, during a rare summer thunderstorm, a fire broke loose in the forest. It came when a sword of lightning struck a tall tree with blistering swiftness. The hungry flames that started in this one tree crawled over its entire body and consumed all its leaves.

The fire continued to spread, leaping with the dry wind onto the surrounding trees and plants. It moved as deftly as the lightning that gave it birth.

The young tree shivered, wishing she could flee, just as she saw the animals of the forest doing. Yet, when she observed how the great tree, along with all the redwoods around her stood stoically calm and unafraid, she knew she must join them in their stance, gathering all the courage she could muster, as she felt the flames of fire begin to lick the base of her trunk.

As the fire tried to penetrate her tough, thick, fibrous bark, it began to lose its strength for a lack of fuel and air. The young redwood was grateful for her moist bark, which proved extremely resistant to fire. It was made up of dead and aging cells, which contained tannin. The tannin was not only an insect repellent, but now she saw that her bark was also a natural fire retardant.

Soon the fire died, since it could no longer compete with the cool dampness of the redwood forest. As for the young redwood tree, only half of her outer bark got charred on one side of her trunk, while the cambium right inside was only slightly damaged. She was relieved that she came out all right, relieved that her fellow larger trees all survived this fire, and very glad it was finally over. And after the fire came two unique feelings that she had never experienced before.

First, she discovered what faith was, seeing that in time the forest would heal again and flourish. In time she would grow new bark over the cave-like scar in her skin. But besides learning faith, she somehow strangely felt stronger from surviving the fire, more powerful than she had ever felt before.

Chapter X

The young redwood had seen over 60 springs, and was well over 50 feet tall now. Her bark was growing thicker and more fibrous, while the new layers of sapwood kept adding width. Her continuously changing form had brought her to the first stages of grace and grandeur that belong to well-aged redwood trees. But her own blooming beauty was nothing to compare with the trees that stood around her. They were, in fact, even more beautiful to her now than when she was a newborn seedling.

The forest was lush, teeming with plant life and animal activity. The young tree never lost her fascination as she witnessed the mating rituals among the animals, and then the miracle of birth taking place! Though she had seen this cycle of life and birth for over 60 years, she still felt moved with appreciation for the ongoing, regenerative powers of life.

She had also observed, with wonder, the changes taking place in her human friend Chipmunk who came to stop by almost every year. Now, so many years older, he was beginning to look more and more like the great-grandmother the young redwood would always remember with fondness. Now her Chipmunk, who was once so straight a young man, was growing ancient, bent, yet graceful. And on this particular day, just like so long ago, he brought his own grandson to stand between one of the grandest trees of the forest and the young tree.

"Look up at these trees," Chipmunk said, putting his arm around his grandson's shoulder. "May we continue like them and learn from their greatness, my son."

"I remember the prayer you taught me, Grandfather," the young boy said earnestly;

"Let me hear it, Son," he smiled affectionately.

"Earth teach me stillness
As the grasses are stilled with light.
Earth teach me suffering
As old stones suffer with memory.
Earth teach me humility
As blossoms are humble with beginning.
Earth teach me caring
As the mother who secures her young.
Earth teach me courage
As the tree which stands alone.
Earth teach me limitation
As the ant which crawls on the ground.
Earth teach me freedom
As the eagle which soars in the sky.
Earth teach me regeneration
As the seed which rises in the spring.
Earth teach me to forget myself
As melted snow forgets its life.
Earth teach me to remember kindness
As dry fields weep with rain."

"Chipmunk, my friend, you have learned all these things from the Earth," the young tree wanted to say as she watched, with fondness and pain, her human companion walk away with his grandson.

The young tree was beginning to understand the cycle of life and death with more clarity. She understood the aging process since she had observed nature's way for so many years now. She had seen Chipmunk grow from a boy to an old man. She knew that Chipmunk's time was coming. He would soon entrust his spirit and body completely to the infinite Mother Earth who would eventually take and channel and mold his life into new life. His body would return to the earth, decompose and become food for other new life.

Her own body was following this same cycle. Although she was still very young, only 65 years old, her body was mature enough to continue the cycle of life. Each year, since the time she had turned 20 years of age, she produced thousands of seed cones, each containing 60 seeds. Her own body also manufactured pollen cones so that the seeds could be germinated, so that new life could spring from her abundance.

Of course, very few seedlings that sprang from her were successful. The majority of seedlings eventually died, either from fungal attack, or from the inability to penetrate the duff covering the forest floor. But the young tree had hopes for the few who did survive. In time, if they continued to grow, she could help them. Already she had begun to extend her roots out to them, just as was done for her when she was young.

These seedlings were a part of her, just as much as the other surrounding redwood trees.

Seed cone

Pollen cone

Well over three hundred years passed and strange changes began to occur, changes that the growing redwood tree could not understand, but would be forced to accept over the next two centuries.

She saw the Ohlone people come less and less often, until it seemed they vanished altogether. And while she witnessed their gradual disappearance, she also saw another people come to take their place. These people had fair skin, and their hair and their style of clothing were very different.

They came to touch the skin of the redwood trees, with eyes that held admiration, but no reverence; with hands that carried no acorn baskets, but axes.

The growing redwood tree was just over 170 feet tall, tall enough to see far across the river and watch these men come, first with long hand-saws and axes; and then later, as the years passed, with power saws and mighty bulldozers. Although these tools and machines were so much smaller than the redwood trees, they wreaked greater destruction than any fire or flood.

Across the river, the growing redwood tree witnessed thousands of redwoods slaughtered until she saw a wasted land. Many of the animals lost their homes. Many of the grizzly bears, the guardians of the forest, were shot and killed until finally they became extinct in the redwood forest. The mountain lions suffered nearly the same fate. Because of the destruction of the large trees, the shade-loving plants were now exposed to full sunlight. Soon, they died off too.

Eventually, these same men, with their powerful machines, would make their way across the river and continue to assault the forest. Each day, the growing redwood tree could feel the reverberations of the power saws and bulldozers grow stronger and closer. She could not only feel the vibrations coming from the saws' blades, but she could feel the final groaning, piercing cracks coming from the falling trees. One day she also watched, from only 30 yards away, how these men so swiftly felled a tree only slightly younger than she. It had stood so proud, so straight and tall. Now it stood no more.

The men were not quite through with their day's work. They finally came to inspect the circle of ancient trees where the growing redwood stood. They eagerly eyed one of the largest trees of the forest, the one who had first curled its roots around the young tree's own.

"This is a fine old-growth tree," one man called out with glee. "She'll be worth plenty of lumber... plenty of money!" he grinned. "Let's cut her down and then call it quits for the day, what d'ya say, men?" he shouted.

And so, it was on this day that the growing redwood saw her friend, the first tree who took her roots into her own, fall. She was stripped, cut into large pieces, and hauled off by the trucks.

Unable to fight back, unable to defend her friends and forest community, the young redwood felt her courage fade. The young tree could have cried.

She looked up at the circle of remaining trees standing as stoically as ever, brave till the bitter end. And as she gazed at them, she knew she must do the same. For the sake of her great tree friend, for the sake of her forest community, for the sake of her human friends, the Ohlone people whom she sensed were perhaps slaughtered like these trees, she knew she must maintain her pride and dignity, in spite of the great emptiness and sorrow that filled her tree spirit.

Chapter XII

Heavy rains followed the death of the growing tree's old-growth friend. No white men had shown up for weeks in this stripped forest where countless rows of redwood stumps marked out the remains of the destroyed community, like thousands of nameless tombstones.

Shortly after the rains ended, only a handful of humans trickled into this desolate graveyard. But these fair-skinned humans carried no axe or power saw. They came with empty hands and lowered heads. They came and stood close to where one of the tallest of redwood trees had stood. A short, stocky man counted the number of sapwood rings on a stump and told the people around him that this tree had lived for over a thousand years. Then a tall, slender, distinguished-looking man pulled out from his coat pocket a copy of a letter written in 1852 by a man named Chief Seattle, of the Dwanish-Squqamish people of the Pacific Northwest.

The tall man cleared his throat and said, "I have managed to get a copy of this letter. Please listen to its words carefully as I read it to you. It says:

"The president in Washington sends word that he wishes to buy our land. But how can you buy or sell the sky? The Land? The idea is strange to us. If we do not own the freshness of the air and the sparkle of the water, how can you buy them?

"Every Part of this Earth is sacred to my people. Every shining pine needle, every sandy shore, every mist in the dark woods, every meadow, every humming insect. All are holy in the memory and experience of my people.

"We know the sap which courses through the trees as we know the blood that courses through our veins. We are part of the Earth and it is part of us. The perfumed flowers are our sisters. The bear, the deer, the great eagle, these are our brothers. The rocky crests, the juices in the meadow, the body heat of the pony, the man, all belong to the same family.

"The shining water that moves in the streams and rivers is not just water, but the blood of our ancestors. If we sell you our land, you must remember that it is sacred. Each ghostly reflection in the clear waters of the lakes tells of events and memories in the life of my people. The water's murmur is the voice of my father's father.

"The rivers are our brothers. They quench our thirst. They carry our canoes and feed our children. So you must give to the rivers the kindness you would give any brother.

"If we sell you our land, remember that the air is precious to us, that the air shares its spirit with all the life it supports. The wind that gave our grandfather his first breath also receives his last sigh. The wind also gives our children the spirit of life. So if we sell you our land, you must keep it apart and sacred, as a place where many can go to taste the wind that is sweetened by the meadow flowers.

"Will you teach your children what we have taught our children? That the Earth is our Mother?

What befalls the Earth befalls the sons of the Earth.

"This we know: the Earth does not belong to man, man belongs to the Earth. All things are connected like the blood that unites us all. Man did not weave the web of life; he is merely a strand in it. Whatever he does to the web, he does to himself.

"Your destiny is a mystery to us. What will happen when the buffalo are all slaughtered? The wild horses tamed? What will happen when the secret corners of the forest are heavy with the scent of many men and the view of the ripe hills is blotted out by talking wires? Where will the thicket be? Gone! Where will the eagle be? Gone! And what is it to say goodbye to the swift pony and the hunt? The end of living and the beginning of survival.

"When the last red man has vanished with his wilderness and his memory is only the shadow of a cloud moving across the prairie, will these shores and forests still be here? Will there be any of the spirit of my people left?

"We love this Earth as a newborn loves its mother's heartbeat. So, if we sell you our land, love it as we have loved it. Care for it as we have cared for it. Hold in your mind the memory of the land as it is when you receive it. Preserve the land for all children and love it, as God loves us all.

"As we are part of the land, you too are part of the land. This Earth is precious to us. It is also precious to you. One thing we know: there is only one god. No man, be he red man or white man, can be apart. We are brothers after all."

When he finished reading this letter, another man spoke up and began to read to the handful of listening humans a poem that he admired, and the growing redwood continued to listen intently, remembering with pain her Ohlone friends.

"We have forgotten who we are,
We have alienated ourselves from the unfolding
Of the cosmos.
We have become estranged from the movements
Of the Earth.
We have turned our backs on the cycles of life.

We have forgotten who we are.

We have sought only our own security.
We have exploited simply for our own ends.
We have distorted our knowledge.
We have abused our power.

We have forgotten who we are.

Now the land is barren,
And the waters are poisoned,
And the air is polluted.

We have forgotten who we are.

Now the forests are dying,
And the creatures are disappearing,
And the humans are despairing.

We have forgotten who we are.
We ask forgiveness.

We ask for the gift of remembering.
We ask for the strength to change.

We have forgotten who we are."

After he concluded the poem, the gathering unanimously agreed that they must fight to protect the remaining redwood trees. They also agreed not to stop or surrender in this fight until the life of these remaining coastal forest communities was secure.

After hearing these words, the growing tree felt a surge of hope course through her sapwood, but her hope was short-lived. A week later the other men came back. They were the men with the power saws in their hands. They began cutting down more trees, and their voices sounded angry.

The tree realized through their exchange of heated words that there was a fight between the nature conservationists and the tree cutters. These loggers were fearful of losing their jobs, and worried about how they were going to feed their families.

The tree grieved over their concerns. There must be a better solution, she thought to herself. But are my life and the life of the forest community so unimportant that you

humans would continue to destroy us all to support your own kind? You do not know that you need us in a way that exceeds the value of our physical bodies. I am a vital part of the whole in this chain of life. As a part of all living plants, I provide you with oxygen so that you will not die! And by my existence as only one tree of the redwood community, my very life calls and gathers the rain clouds, so that you can have water!

The tree continued in her own thought, troubled, angry, and sad, as the men continued working. She wondered if those other people would ever come back and deliver the rest of the redwood forest from these loggers' hands.

Suddenly her thoughts were interrupted by a discussion held by two men. They were staring up at one tree who had two smaller trees growing out heavy branches emerging from her upper trunk, about eighty feet up.

"We could get three suckers out of this one, huh?" said the younger man.

"No, Um. Well...no," the older man shook his head.

"Why not?" demanded the younger man.

The elder did not respond right away as he kept looking at this tree.

"Well, why not?" the young man insisted.

"Maybe I'm superstitious," the older man finally answered, "but we can't kill this one. It's got two trees coming out of it like arms reaching up to heaven. It's as if the tree was praying." He hesitated. "No. Leave it go. We can find another tree."

The younger man shook his head and said nothing while the other led him to the growing tree.

They stopped right in front of her, ready to cut her down. She felt the saw even before it touched her. The growing redwood tree's life was over.

The elder man started up his power saw. Just the shrill buzzing sound it gave off made the tree feel sick inside with dread. But she knew she must continue to be as brave as she could in the face of death.

ꕤ Chapter XIII ꕤ

Before the older man and his partner could touch her bark with their power saw, another short, stocky man with a thick curly beard came near and yelled, "Come on! Quitting time! It's payday! Let's get a beer."

A strong wind blew. The tree creaked and groaned. Her whole body seemed to sigh with the wind.

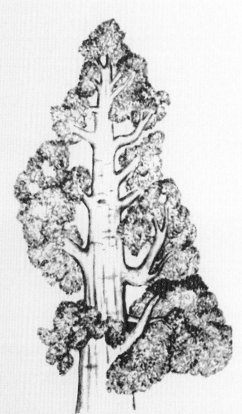

Chapter XIV

Weeks passed. No lumberjacks showed up on the remaining forest site. Only a few families came. Among them were some women who were pregnant. Their stomachs were large and heavy, like the protruding burls that sometimes grew on redwoods.

The growing tree remembered with happy thoughts the Ohlone women who used to look the same way at times, until they gave birth to their human sprouts. The tree, herself, also had a few small redwood sprouts growing from her own body. As the growing tree reminisced over her past Ohlone friends, her thoughts returned to the present as one young woman began to speak to her daughter.

"Listen my daughter," the woman smiled with pride. "Our group has bought this land from the logging company. This is your forest and mine now, to respect and cherish. This forest will be preserved for you and your children, and your children's children...for all children forever."

Then they sat together on a large stump while the mother began to read her daughter a poem.

"To The Redwood Tree

Such a tiny seed,
Seemingly insignificant,
Cast invisible against the hard ground.
Abandoned,
Left to her own means of survival.
Who could have ever imagined life
Springing from this speck of dust?

But marvel still further
At her strength and power,
For inside she has the will of a giant.
Pushing her way through,
Pushing her way up higher and higher,
Even breaking apart cement,
So that even man's power cannot
Suppress her will to thrive!

Stretching, growing ever upward,
Until she reaches full stature,
Until someday we might glimpse her
Holy and magnificent posture.
A spirit of the forest acting on our behalf,
Intercessor between humans and the clouds of rain."

As the woman read, suddenly the tree grew excited. She hadn't noticed until this moment that growing from the stump of her once oldest, largest, most beautiful friend, sprang new saplings.

If the growing redwood tree could have laughed with joy she would have, for she saw at this moment how wonderfully tenacious life is, determined to survive even under the bleakest conditions.

The ancient circle of trees that she had known for some 565 years would continue to live and keep growing. She, too, would keep growing, together with her own few offspring. One day, she would be among the largest trees. But more than that, she would gather and protect the new roots of her friend's progeny, into her own.

REDWOOD TREE ANATOMY & ECOLOGY

I'd like to share with you a little more about the anatomy of the redwood tree in this story. To begin with, when she was only a seedling, it was easy for her to transfer all the nutrient-rich water she needed from the soil. By means of pressure that built up inside her roots as they absorbed water, the water was forced to travel upward. This root-pressured system is similar to the way Redwoodfern filled one of the deer-skinned pouches with water.

At first the waterproof pouch merely expanded from the bottom, as the skin stretched out. But as Redwoodfern continued to fill it, the skin eventually could stretch no more, and so the water inside had to rise to the very top of the pouch.

But once the redwood sapling grew, her roots could only expand enough to force the water and minerals about two feet up her body through her **xylem.** (The xylem, a set of tube-like structures inside a tree's roots, trunk, and branches, acts as a food and water conductor, similar to the way the arteries and veins function to move blood within human and animal bodies.) So to assist this pushing work done by the roots, she needed a pulling force to bring water up through the xylem, which she felt take place in her needle-like leaves.

Her leaves, which contained high amounts of **photosynthesized** sugars, used some of the sugars as energy to draw up water through her xylem, similar to the way we take in foods that our bodies convert into sugars and then store in our body's cells, until we use them as energy to work, play, or make things. When the leaves use energy to draw up water, the water is stored in tissues called **mesophyll** inside her leaves, which by the sun's heat, changes into vapor. This vapor fills the mesophyll, until unneeded water escapes from tiny openings called **stomata** in her leaves.

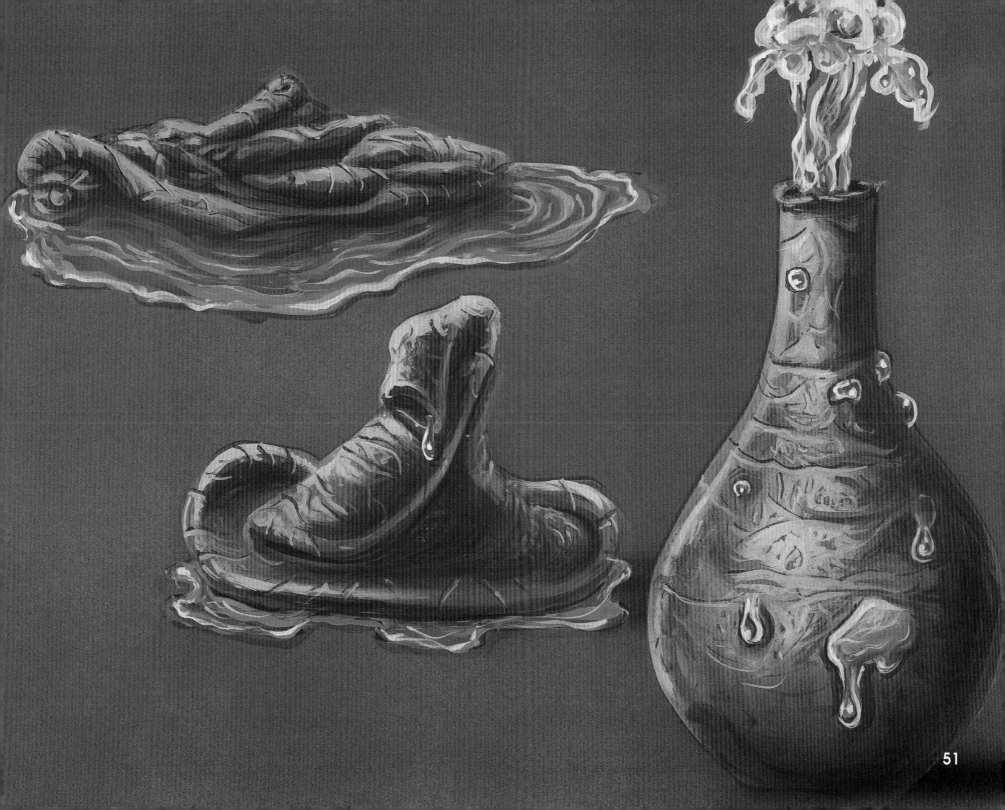

This entire process, which is called **Xylem** from a straw every day!

transpiration, is comparable to the way we perspire when we get too hot. Our sweat is able to escape through our skin's pores, little holes similar to the stomata in a leaf. But, unlike us, the vaporized water lost from a tree's leaves is always immediately replaced by the water pulled through her xylem by the mesophyll cells in the leaves. We might compare the mesophyll to our lips, and the connected xylem of roots, trunk and stems, as a straw to drink from. The only difference is that the drawing or sucking force, called **transpirational pull,** is so strong, it can pull between 100 to 500 gallons of water a day throughout the entire length of the tree! Imagine what it would be like if we drank that much water

Now let's take a closer look at another aspect of the redwood tree's anatomy; the layers and functions of the wood. If we were to take a cross section of her trunk, we would see that she is made up of five main layers that help give her strength, protection, and the ability to move water and nutrients from roots to leaves and bark. The outer layer of the tree is the bark: the skin of the tree, that gives protection to the living, active layers of cells just beneath. The first of these is called the **phloem,** a layer of tubes that carry sugars produced by the leaves to the rest of the tree. The next layer is the **cambium,** a very narrow ring of living cells that produce not only new layers of bark to the tree each year, but also, new layers of phloem and xylem cells. Inside the cell-producing cambium layer, are the xylem cells, or **sapwood,** that carry water, minerals and sap up from the roots with the

Water molecules

transpirational pull of the leaves. Older, inner sapwood cells become tougher and less active in moving water, since their fibrous chambers become stronger and more dense or thick. It would be like trying to drink water through a clogged straw. Inner sapwood cells eventually become part of the innermost layer of the tree's trunk, the **heartwood.** The heartwood consists of tough but non-living, inactive cells that give the tree its strength. The heartwood is almost like the skeletons within our own bodies that allow us to stand tall.

Each separate, apparent needle growing from the redwood tree's stems is an actual leaf! So redwood trees have thousands of little leaves. All these leaves are needed to pull those 100 to 500 gallons of water throughout the length of the tree daily.

Redwood trees have two kinds of cones, the female and the male seed cone. Both seed cones are needed to produce new trees. Redwoods can also produce new trees by sprouting from existing stumps or roots.

Transpiration

Photosynthesis is the process by which the tree makes sugar to nourish itself. It is similar to the way Redwoodfern and her Ohlone companions made bread from acorn flour. To make bread, she needed to mix acorn flour and boiled water together, then bake the mixture on a heated flat rock.

The leaves in trees and plants mix water and the minerals from the soil together with a gas they draw in from the air, called carbon dioxide (the gas that we exhale or breathe out into our atmosphere). Then the leaves use the light from the sun, and water, to make their own food in the form of sugar. As the leaves in trees and plants produce sugar, they release oxygen into the air, the gas we breathe in and depend on to live. So there is an exchange of these essential gases between plants and animals that is needed for continued life on our planet.

Over the past hundred years, we have come to understand and appreciate the vital importance of our forests. We have learned how their root systems, by holding the soil they grow in, protect our land from destructive erosion from rain and runoff water. We have learned how the trees provide food and shelter for many animals. We have also come to understand how their leaves act as a filter that constantly cleans our air of harmful gases, while simultaneously producing life-sustaining oxygen for all animals. The ocean plays the major role in creating and maintaining our water cycle; yet, the tall, old growth trees also play a significant part in creating rain clouds, because they exhale water vapor from which clouds are made. While we still depend on wood to make our homes, this awareness has moved many lumber companies to conserve the forests they harvest. Rather than destroying entire forests through clear cutting practices, as they did in the past, they have begun to use selective cutting techniques. They preserve most of the old growth trees in a forest, harvest the most useable mid-size trees, and remove the congested undergrowth to make room for the smaller, younger trees to grow. This practice of selective cutting ultimately promotes a healthier forest, and reduces the chance of any wildfires getting out of hand and completely destroying a forest.

Some of these logging companies are also trying to further promote the growth of redwoods by replacing the trees they cut with saplings. Some of the logging industry's efforts to protect our forests are helping our planet's health. However, environmental groups are still finding it crucial to fight for our rapidly diminishing old-growth and rain forests, because the growing human population demands that more cities and homes be built. Our forests are also in danger from global warming, and by continued clear-cutting of forests by some logging companies, especially in countries outside the U.S. Both logging companies that promote conservational practices, and environmentalists, keenly realize that we all need to take greater responsibility to preserve, protect, and cherish our forests and oceans, indeed our entire planet.

Hope of the Future

To the children, the seeds of the future.
May they have the courage to live their dream,
To know truth in their hearts,
To cherish intrinsic knowledge in their mind,
To seek a sense of purpose in their souls,
To feel joy throughout their bodies,
To protect precious life on this planet,
through each person's relationship with the earth.
May they understand the importance of the forests
And clear running streams,
The rights of all creatures, great and small.
To be compassionate,
To show and maintain the courage of their convictions,
A concern for life,
The pride of the present,
The hope of the future.

— Paul Gaylon

OTHER BOOKS WRITTEN BY THIS AUTHOR

Lacy's Journey: The Life of a Decorator Crab   (coming 2009)

(soon to be published)

Atoms Matter

The Life of Bobby Kennedy Jr.

Tell Me About The Little Brown Bat

Amigito: A story about the life cycle of the Monarch butterflies

The Cat Who Wanted to Walk

---

*A special note about the poems interweaved in the story: Chief Dan George wrote the first poem in chapter 3. Starhawk, author of *The Spiral Dance* and other books, wrote the second poem, in chapter 7. The third poem, in chapter 10, is actually a prayer written by a Ute Indian. An unknown author wrote the fourth poem in chapter 12 from the U.S. Environmental Sabbath Program. I wrote the last poem in chapter 14.

AFTERWORD

Some readers have questioned why I chose to anthropomorphize the redwood tree in a story that is otherwise scientifically based. In answer, I share my perspective as a teacher. One of the most effective ways I can help my students understand and retain information is to present it through a story that involves a protagonist with whom they can personally identify. Once students' hearts are engaged in the joys and challenges faced by that character, their natural curiosity is sparked to learn more about the subject the story character personifies. Teaching through the use of anthropomorphism, can also draw children into a sympathetic appreciation for messages about life and death.

However, my decision to give a voice to the redwood tree originally sprang from musings shared with me by both friends and strangers. Hiking the state park, I often heard people wonder, "If trees could talk, what might they say?" I would look up at those grand redwood trees, and ponder some of the poetry I had read, guessing about the consciousness and wisdom of these living beings; and I, too, began to wonder: If they could speak, what would these old trees, who have lived hundreds, if not thousands of years, say about their experience of life?

At Cabrillo Community College, I took a course in Native American history and learned that many Native Americans believed that all plants and animals were their brothers and sisters. Through their strong sense of kinship to the natural world around them, came a respectful understanding of how nature benefited and protected people. Their dependence on the earth's natural resources to sustain them led them to regard the earth as their mother, so that they learned, not to conquer, but co-exist with nature. I came to believe that if we used our advanced technology in ways that incorporated a respectful and appreciative relationship with our earth, even as many Native Americans still advocate, then we could save our planet's bounty of life and beauty.

Later, when I took a plant biology course at San Jose State University, I was struck by how similar trees and plants are to us. I learned about the ways the trees, like us, have systems of tube-like channels for moving water l nutrients throughout their bodies; and about the ways in which the plants procreate, live, protect themselves, grow old, acquire diseases, and die. Then, years later, I read a book entitled, *The Secret Life of Plants,* written by Peter Tompkins and Christopher Bird, that used extensive research to show evidence that plants are sentient.

As I reflected on these findings, and what I had learned about the Native Americans' relationship with nature, I felt compelled to act on behalf of our remaining redwood forests. I found myself asking once again, "If trees could talk, what would they tell us?" After walking on the trails of California's coastal redwood forests for so many years, I have come to know some of these redwood trees individually by their own distinct physical characteristics, and have developed such an affinity, gratitude, and respect towards these special trees, that somehow I felt as if I knew what they might say. I felt as if the trees were telling me what to say as I wrote this story.

ABOUT THE ILLUSTRATOR

I have been a professional freelance artist for over thirty years, running my own shop, Clownbank Studio, and creating illustrations, murals, and fine art signs for numerous individuals and businesses. I specialize in airbrushing and hand painting, and have worked on such diverse projects as painting carousel horses for Disney and Universal Studio Tours, book and CD covers, portraits, and editorial illustrations for magazines as well as murals for Buck Owens Productions, the cities of Santa Clarita, Santa Cruz, Chico, Paradise, Salt Lake City, Sacramento, and Watsonville. Although I use many digital tools in my work, I love to paint in the analog world.

I was born on boring Long Island, New York, in 1951, and attended prestigious Pratt Institute in New York City from 1968-72, and then fled to San Francisco in 1972 where for four years I was a street artist airbrushing T-shirts on Fisherman's Wharf. Over the years, I honed my skills

and picked up clients such as Silicon Graphics, Atari, Buck Owens Productions, Dell Publishing, and many others.

Painting the art for *A VOICE FOR THE REDWOODS* was a four year labor of love. Inspired by Loretta's writing and her mission to save the redwoods, I saw an excellent opportunity to put the full force of my talent behind this worthy cause.

I currently live in Paradise, California with my dog Domino. You can see more of my work at my website www.clownbank.com. I am available for commissions.

ABOUT THE AUTHOR

I was born and raised in Burbank, CA, but I have lived and hiked in the Santa Cruz Mountains, under the beauty of their great redwoods, since moving to this area at age 19. Twelve years ago, during a difficult period in my life, I walked into Henry Cowell Redwoods State Park to begin my usual walk through its old growth forest. I came and stood before my favorite tree, that I named Eyesa. Knowing I was losing my youth, feeling a lack of direction and purpose in my life, I stood there before Eyesa, feeling quite sorry for myself, until I heard what seemed like this tree's voice beckoning me to come closer to her. I nestled inside a wide crevice in her trunk, pressed my ear against her and listened. A voice went off inside my head, "Do you dare tell me, Eyesa, how ugly you feel about yourself?"

I gazed up at this grand and gnarled tree that reminded me so much of a frozen waterfall cascading gracefully downward into the heart of the earth. That same voice challenged me again. Humbled by the spirit and wisdom of this tree, perhaps, I thought, an angel in tree form, I had to acknowledge her perception of all life—that all creatures, great and small, possess beauty, grace and

purpose. I did not know what my purpose was yet, until four years later, while earning my degree and teaching credential at San Jose State University.

Once again I came back to Eyesa, as I had done so many times before, only this time I uttered a prayer and made a vow before this tree, to help protect our forests by teaching children about ecology. Inspired by this tree, I conceived this story. Around the same time, my hopes of becoming an environmentally based schoolteacher became a reality. I am currently teaching sixth grade at Seven Trees Elementary in San Jose, California, a school named after the seven young redwoods that are growing on its campus.

If you'd like to meet Eyesa yourself, go to Henry Cowell Redwoods State Park in Felton, California, and walk the loop trail near the main parking lot. Eyesa is Number 11 of the marked trees on the loop, a huge old tree with extensive burls growing around her trunk. May she bring you inspiration, as she did me.